The
Anti-Social Network

A Place For All The Thoughts, Ideas And Plans
You Don't Want To Share 👍

Brought to you by Marc Hartzman

Cur*i*ous
PUBLICATIONS

ISBN-10: 0615539785
Library of Congress Control Number: 2011938650

Curious Publications
101 W. 23rd St. #318
New York, NY 10011

curiouspublications.com

Printed and bound in the United States.

User Name

_____

Contact Information

Dear **Friend,**

I hope you don't mind that I've called you a friend, even though we've never met. Of course, if you're anything like the more than 500 million people on Facebook, you're probably quite used to being friends with people you've never met, barely know, or knew 20 years ago.

Sure, Facebook and other social networking sites have their benefits. They can inform in an instant, create useful connections, and entertain. But they can also become addictive and suck you into a vast wasteland of nothingness. The majority of posts and tweets are frivolous nonsense. People say things to everyone they would've never bothered telling anyone in person before—like what they're eating right now, what they think of the weather, where they're going tonight, and more than we really need to know about nearly everything else.

Our personal lives have become public. And everyone is ok with this. It's like Big Brother pulled a practical joke on civilization and no one's caught on.

Except, perhaps, you. You, my friend of almost two minutes, who purchased this book as a place to share absolutely nothing. A place where your thoughts are yours and will stay that way.

Thank you, friend, for joining The Anti-Social Network. I'll leave you alone now.

- Marc Hartzman

Sketch your profile picture here ⟩

Look! Your own personal page. 200 of them.

999,999,999 fewer users than Facebook.

Write 140 characters. Better yet, draw 140 characters.

Privacy Settings: Do not share, do not lose.

Terms of Service: The Anti-Social Network provides pages to write on. You write on them.

Recent activity:

To post photos, upload with tape.

Spend less time online and you'll have more to write about.

Carry this book and it becomes a mobile version.

Retweets are no substitute for original thinking.

Bookmark this page by inserting a bookmark.

Shred page to delete.

Updated ___ seconds ago.

Flip pages to search.

You are not wasting time on FarmVille®.

User generated content:

At this moment, you are not making Mark Zuckerberg any richer.

Like birds, people who tweet are mostly full of crap.

Friend someone in person today.

Things you like without clicking a button that says so:

Here, #hashtags are for playing Tic Tac Toe.

This book offers one location-based service: It won't tell anyone where you are.

No character limit:

Trending:

Those who share everything are just selfish for attention.

OMG, u should nvr have 2 write like this.

No one from high school will bother you here.

Gain followers with the strength of your ideas, not the number of your tweets.

To tag this page, fold the corner.

Employers will never see embarrassing details.

No book ever spread a virus.

To send a message: Remove page, insert into envelope, affix stamp.

To crowdsource an answer, ask a question out loud.

Instagram does not make you an insta-professional.

Create your own News Feed:

For GPS services, draw a map:

If people really had an average of 150 friends, they wouldn't have so much time to spend online.

There's no app for this.

Easy to read in sunlight.

No memories will be sold to marketers.

Save the Fail Whale. Tweet less.

To view all comments, read all pages.

Birthdays (of people you would expect to say Happy Birthday to):

Name _____ Date _____

Name _____ Date _____

Name _____ Date _____

Name _____ Date _____

Name _____ Date _____

Name _____ Date _____

Name _____ Date _____

Name _____ Date _____

Name _____ Date _____

Name _____ Date _____

Name _____ Date _____

Name _____ Date _____

Name _____ Date _____

Name _____ Date _____

Name _____ Date _____

Name _____ Date _____

Name _____ Date _____

Name _____ Date _____

Name _____ Date _____

Name _____ Date _____

Name _____ Date _____

Name _____ Date _____

Name _____ Date _____

Name _____ Date _____

Name _____ Date _____

Name _____ Date _____

Name _____ Date _____

Name _____ Date _____

Name _____ Date _____

Name _____ Date _____

Check-ins are for hotels.

Don't poke anyone.

Wifi unavailable. Please enjoy unlimited focus.

Chat with someone face to face.

Update your profile picture

Do not express yourself with an emoticon.

You are now connected to no one.

Telephones still work.

No one needs to know what you're doing right now.

48% of people check Facebook right when they wake up. The rest of us start our day.

You are not the mayor of anything.

Badges are for Boy Scouts.

Anti-Social Graph Paper

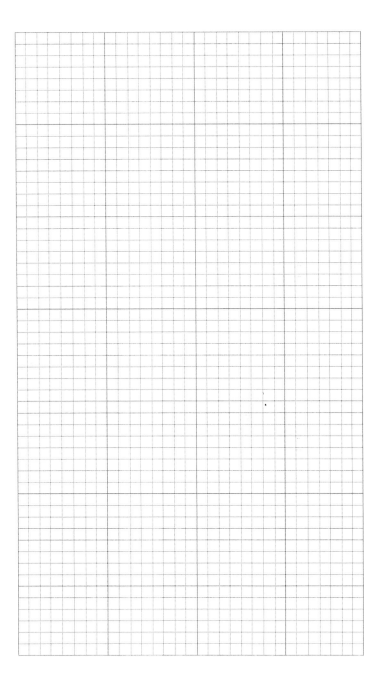

The Twitterverse will never be as interesting as the universe.

To see what your friends are doing, spend time with them.

Sketch something. Instagram nothing.

No ads here.

_____

Or here.

_____

Not even here.

_____

Write something amazing and you can blog about it later.

0 friends like this. Because 0 friends know about this.

Forget your password.

Attach a file with a real paper clip.

No one will add an unflattering photo of you from ten years ago.

This book will not suggest other books you might like.

Unfollow. In other words, lead.

Write a comment. Originate a thought. Develop an insight. Muster an idea. Hatch a plan.

More private than your obsolete Myspace page.

To ignore, close book.

If you want to be social, go out.

People on Facebook spend 700 billion minutes a month not reading literature.

Living vicariously is not living.

If you want your life to be public, run for office.

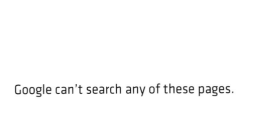

Google can't search any of these pages.

Not a single scam. Unless you didn't expect this book to be virtually blank.

Notification: This is the end of the book.

Made in the USA
San Bernardino, CA
11 April 2014